HIGH TIDE

Celebrating another Alabama Crimson Tide National Championship

Book design by **ANDREA ZAGATA**

ISBN: 978-1-940056-90-6

Printed in the United States of America

INTRODUCTION

Alabama Crimson Tide – National Champions!

Sounds pretty good doesn't it? Alabama fans have waited three long years to utter those words, and now, the Crimson Tide are back on top.

Let the celebration begin!

This was a championship 12 months in the making. After two heartbreaking losses to LSU and Auburn kept the Crimson Tide out of the 2019 college football playoffs, Coach Nick Saban and the returning Alabama players headed into the offseason with one goal in mind—winning a national championship in 2020.

In a season with unprecedented challenges due to the Covid-19 epidemic, the Crimson Tide kept a laser-like focus on the task at hand.

Led by one of the most prolific and talented offenses in the history of the sport—the Tide offense featured five All-Americans, including Heisman Trophy winner DeVonta Smith and two more players (quarterback Mac Jones and running back Najee Harris) who finished in the top five in Heisman voting—Bama rolled through the SEC by scoring 50 or more points in six of their 11 conference games. An opportune defense adept at rising to the occasion solidified this Alabama team as one of the greatest in the school's storied history.

In the following pages enjoy a trip down memory lane of this incredible championship season that came to its jubilant conclusion with the National Championship game victory in Miami over a very talented Ohio State team.

Knowing everything his players had to endure this season, Saban couldn't be any prouder of his team.

"Our team has shown a lot of maturity and perseverance throughout the season," Saban said. "We told our players all year that the team that shows the maturity to be able to handle disruptions is going to have the best chance to be successful in the end. We were able to do that. I'm very proud of what this group has been able to accomplish."

NATIONAL CHAMPIONS!

No. 1 Alabama wins national title 52-24 over No. 3 Ohio State

Jan 11, 2021

Miami Gardens, Fla. — DeVonta Smith was uncoverable, Najee Harris unstoppable and Mac Jones impeccable. With a performance that was both surgical and explosive, No. 1 Alabama won the College Football Playoff national championship game 52-24 against No. 3 Ohio State on Monday night.

The final game of a college football season in a pandemic, a season that was uncertain to be played in the summer and filled with disruptions in the fall, ended in the most predictable fashion: Alabama (13-0) as national champion for the sixth time in the last 12 years under coach Nick Saban.

For Saban, it was career title No. 7 overall, breaking a tie with Alabama great Paul "Bear" Bryant for the most by a major college coach.

"To me this is the ultimate team," Saban said. "There is more togetherness on this team than on almost any team we've ever had. They've had to overcome and to persevere so much through this season, and they have done it magnificently."

The celebration was at once familiar and unique. The confetti cannons sent a crimson and white shower into the air and the Tide players ran to the sideline to grab their championship hats and T-shirts. It's a rite of passage if you have played for Saban.

But this time, the band playing the fight song was a piped in recording and when "Sweet Home Alabama" blared, only a few thousand Tide fans were still in the building to singalong.

The Buckeyes fans were mostly long gone.

Ohio State (7-1) just couldn't keep up. Justin Fields, playing what might be his last game before heading to the NFL, passed for 194 yards and a touchdown. Whether Fields was 100% after taking a brutal hit to the side during his brilliant semifinal performance against Clemson was hard to know for sure.

On the Buckeyes' first drive, they lost star running back Trey Sermon to an injury, and in a game they needed to be running at top speed, facing one of great offenses in recent history, they sputtered too much. Ohio State has never allowed more points in a bowl game.

"I think there's a feeling of, if you don't score you're going to get behind and then the pressure mounts," Buckeyes coach Ryan Day said of the Tide's prolific offense.

Fans can debate which team in the Saban dynasty is best, but none will be more memorable than this group.

"Everybody is so together," Smith said. "People last year said the dynasty was over. We don't stop. We just keep reloading."

Alabama coach Nick Saban celebrates with Crimson Tide players after a 52-24 win over Ohio State in the national championship game.

PHOTO BY MICHAEL REAVES/ GETTY IMAGES

Alabama running back Najee Harris runs into the end zone for a first half touchdown against Ohio State. Harris had two scores in a 52-24 national-title win.

AP PHOTO/LYNNE SLADKY

After going a whole two seasons without winning a national title, the Tide finished perfect during a season that could not have been further from it. COVID-19 forced teams into quarantines and endless testing and uncertainty every single week with games played in mostly empty stadiums.

"To me this team accomplished more than almost any team," Saban said. "No disrespect to other teams we had but this team won 11 SEC games. No other team has done that. They won the SEC and went undefeated in the SEC and then they beat two great teams in the playoffs with no break. I think there's going to be quite a bit to write about the legacy of this team."

Only about 15,000 fans were at Hard Rock Stadium, capacity 65,326, to see the last magnificent performance of Smith's college career.

The Heisman Trophy winner had catches for 12 catches for 215 yards and three touchdowns, all in the first half as the Crimson Tide bolted out to a 35-17 lead.

"Heaven's knows what he would have done if he played the whole game," Saban said.

Using an array of motions and misdirections, outgoing offensive coordinator Steve Sarkisian had Ohio State heads spinning trying to track down Smith. At one point, he suddenly was matched up against a linebacker, whom he left in the dust for a 42-yard score with 41 seconds left in the second quarter.

Smith, who finished his freshman season by catching the 2017 national championship winning touchdown pass from Tua Tagovailoa, ended his Alabama career as the leading career receiver in Southeastern Conference history and the most outstanding offensive player of his third title game.

As for Sarkisian, he is on his way to Texas as the head coach. Longhorns fans had to have liked what they saw from their new playcaller. If only he could bring Smith and his fellow Heisman contenders to Austin.

Jones, who finished third in the Heisman voting, was 36 for 45 for a CFP championship-record 464 yards and five touchdowns, operating behind a line that gave him plenty of time. In one of maybe the most overlooked seasons a quarterback has ever played, Jones set a single-season record for passer efficiency rating at 203.

Harris had 158 yards from scrimmage on 29 touches, scoring three times to give him an SEC record 30 touchdowns this season.

Smith hardly played in the second half, leaving with an injury. He returned to the sideline in the fourth quarter with his right hand wrapped to the wrist, two fingers taped together, and wearing a Heisman mask.

Alabama hardly missed him and cracked 50 early in the fourth quarter when Harris went in untouched from a yard out.

Smith and Harris surprised some by returning to college after last season for their senior years.

Boy, did it turn out to be worthwhile. Along with Jones, another member of that 2017 recruiting class, they will leave Alabama as the leaders of a team that managed to make an arduous march from through the pandemic look easy.

"We all had a mission trying to end things the right way," Smith said. We all went to work and it ended the way we wanted."

Alabama linebacker Christopher Allen wraps up Ohio State quarterback Justin Fields during the first half.

AP PHOTO/CHRIS O'MEARA

◄ Najee Harris leaps over a Buckeye defender into the end zone for a first-half touchdown.

AP PHOTO/WILFREDO LEE

▼ Alabama receiver John Metchie III, left, celebrates with DeVonta Smith after Smith scored a touchdown in the title game.

AP PHOTO/CHRIS O'MEARA

▼ Crimson Tide quarterback Mac Jones throws early in the game during Alabama's national championship victory over Ohio State.

AP PHOTO/CHRIS O'MEARA

DeVonta Smith is wide open in front of Ohio State cornerback Shaun Wade on a touchdown reception from Mac Jones in the championship game.

AP PHOTO/WILFREDO LEE

Alabama receiver Slade Bolden stretches across the goal line for a second-half touchdown. It was the first career touchdown for Bolden, a redshirt sophomore.

AP PHOTO/CHRIS O'MEARA

Alabama's Alex Leatherwood holds the trophy for his jubilant teammates during the postgame celebration after the Crimson Tide won the national title.

AP PHOTO/WILFREDO LEE

DELAYED START

No. 2 Crimson Tide rolls on offense to 38-19 win over Mizzou

Sept 26, 2020

COLUMBIA, Mo. — Nick Saban has never lost a season opener while coaching Alabama.

Then again, he'd never had one like this.

Yet despite an offseason largely scrapped by the coronavirus pandemic, and a delayed start to the season, Saban's second-ranked Crimson Tide looked just fine as they began their SEC-only schedule on Saturday night.

Mac Jones threw for 249 yards and two scores in less than three quarters of work, and Jaylen Waddle and Najee Harris had dynamic performances on offense, helping Alabama roll to a 38-19 victory over the rebuilding Tigers.

"I think from a team standpoint, when you play a first game you sort of figure out who you are," Saban said after finally taking off his mask. "You figure out where you and the last thing is, 'What do I have to do to get better?' Everybody on our team has a lot of maturity in what they need to do to get better."

Oh, there are areas to improve. The Crimson Tide had a few too many penalties, a few too many breakdowns on defense and they allowed Missouri to finally get its up-tempo offense going against their backups in the fourth quarter.

They still looked every bit a national title contender, though.

Waddle finished with eight catches for 134 yards and two touchdowns, and Harris ran for 98 yards and three more scores, helping the Crimson Tide spoil the debut of new Tigers coach Eli Drinkwitz and win their 27th straight over the SEC East before a COVID-19-curtailed crowd of 11,738 fans at Faurot Field.

TCU transfer Shawn Robinson, who started for the Tigers over Connor Bazelak, threw for 185 yards and a score. Bazelak also got a few series and was equally ineffective against Dylan Moses, Patrick Surtain II and the rest of the Crimson Tide defense, which kept Drinkwitz's creative offense out of the end zone until midway through the fourth quarter.

Bazelak added a touchdown scamper on the final play of the game for the final margin.

"I saw a lot of fight. I really did," Drinkwitz said. "I thought those guys answered the bell. I don't think it was an issue of not being good enough at all. I thought our guys fought."

Alabama's long wait to start the season actually began with a thud — a three-and-out on offense. But after forcing a three-and-out of their own, Jones began to find his wide receivers downfield and the Crimson Tide got rolling.

At one point, the only question was who was going to score their touchdowns.

Harris had the first on a short plunge and Waddle hauled in 18-yarder for the second a few minutes later. Waddle looked like had another on the Tide's ensuing possession, but a review ruled that he hit the pylon before crossing the goal line and Harris wound up poaching the touchdown for his second of the game.

Waddle eventually got his second, too, when he hauled in a spectacular 23-yard grab in double coverage that sent Alabama into the locker room with a 28-3 lead. In fact, the only slip-up to that point for the Tide came at the end of that play, when Waddle's cleats slipped on the asphalt through the end zone and he landed on his rear.

"Waddle is a great player. He gets open — that's his job — and he does a great job doing it," Jones said. "We've had a great relationship going back to summer, 7-on-7s, getting that chemistry with him, all the late nights at the indoor. He's going to get open and do his job. He makes plays."

Harris added his third touchdown on a twisting 8-yard run early in the second half, allowing Saban to see what freshman quarterback Bryce Young and the rest of their backups could do. They moved the ball in fits and starts, but it was Missouri that finished the game on a high note with a touchdown on the final play.

"We played very well the first half but the second half we need to finish," said Moses, a Butkus Award finalist two years ago who missed all of last season to an injury. "But it's our first game. We just need to improve."

Coach Nick Saban
leads the Crimson Tide
onto the field before
the season opener at
Missouri in September.

AP PHOTO/L.G. PATTERSON

◄ Alabama linebacker Christian Harris celebrates a sack of Missouri quarterback Shawn Robinson during the first quarter.

▼ Running back Najee Harris carries during the first quarter of the season opener

AP PHOTOGRAPHS/L.G. PATTERSON

Wide receiver Jaylen Waddle pulls down a catch between Missouri's Tyree Gillespie, right, and Ishmael Burdine..

AP PHOTO/L.G. PATTERSON

LOOKING FOR A SIGN

Jones throws deep, No. 2 Alabama tops No. 13 Texas A&M 52-24

Oct 3, 2020

TUSCALOOSA, ALA. — Mac Jones launched his first pass far to John Metchie III for a 78-yard touchdown. It was most definitely a sign of things to come.

Jones passed for a career-high 435 yards and four touchdowns, including a pair of deep throws to Metchie and an even longer one to Jaylen Waddle, and No. 2 Alabama romped past No. 13 Texas A&M 52-24 on Saturday.

Briefly threatened early, Jones and the Crimson Tide (2-0) flexed their considerable big-play muscle in the passing game to put away the Aggies (1-1).

"Our guys stayed the course and kept competing in the game," Alabama coach Nick Saban said. "That's really what we wanted to do."

For a team once known for running the ball, Bama aired it out.

Metchie looked like the Tide's latest major receiving threat, alongside Waddle and DeVonta Smith.

Jones topped that initial score with an 87-yard TD to Waddle, who had sprinted past two Aggies defenders to make the grab with nothing but green in between himself and the end zone. Metchie and Jones hooked up for a 63-yarder in the fourth, giving the sophomore five catches for 181 yards.

Waddle said the emerging receiver possesses "sneaky speed."

"He got to showcase that today," he said.

Jones finished 19-of-26 passing for a second straight surgically precise performance marred by one interception off a deflection.

"We won, so it's a good game," Jones said, when asked if it was his best performance.

Waddle had 142 yards receiving and his touchdown catch was tied for the fifth longest in program history, according.

It came after three Alabama penalties in four plays. Jones' three career pass touchdowns of 85-plus yards are the most by a Tide quarterback.

Najee Harris rushed for two short touchdowns and safety Daniel Wright scored on a 47-yard interception return against Kellen Mond.

Mond put up big numbers but it wasn't nearly enough. He completed 25 of 44 passes for 318 yards with three touchdowns — and the pick six. Ainias Smith had six catches for 123 yards and two touchdowns.

"We've got to stop the big plays, learn to be more efficient on offense and take advantage of some more of those opportunities to be able to play and compete," Aggies coach Jimbo Fisher said. "We had some opportunities. I'm disappointed we didn't do it, but there's still a lot to work with, some of our young guys."

But Alabama was off to the races after the Aggies scored two quick first-half touchdowns to tie the game.

"I think guys were shocked that we were right there with them," linebacker Buddy Johnson said.

"And there's no reason to feel that way. It's important that the leaders keep everyone in the moment, stay in the moment and don't get carried away."

Patrick Surtain II reaches to block a pass to Texas A&M's Ryan Renick during the Crimson Tide's 52-24 win in October.

PHOTO BY UA ATHLETICS/ COLLEGIATE IMAGES/GETTY IMAGES

27

Jaylen Waddle runs away
from a flying tackle by
Ainias Smith of Texas
A&M.

*PHOTO BY UA ATHLETICS/
COLLEGIATE IMAGES/GETTY
IMAGES*

HARRIS HAS IT

No. 2 Alabama beats Ole Miss 63-48 in record SEC outburst

Oct 10, 2020

Oxford, Miss. — Lane Kiffin's Mississippi offense put up more yards against an Alabama defense than has ever been done before and scored more points against the Crimson Tide than any unranked team has ever.

It was not enough.

Najee Harris ran for 206 yards and five touchdowns and No. 2 Alabama beat Ole Miss 63-48 on Saturday night in the highest-scoring Southeastern Conference regulation game ever.

Matt Corral passed for 365 yards for Ole Miss (1-2) and the Rebels put up 647 yards on the Tide. The teams combined for an SEC-record 1,370 yards.

"We knew we had to score pretty much every possession," Tide quarterback Mac Jones said.

Alabama and Ole Miss traded touchdowns for much of the night, but with the Tide (3-0) leading 49-42 the Rebels misfired in Alabama territory and had to settle for a field goal. That was as good as a stop in this game. Tide receiver DeVonta Smith went 14 yards for a touchdown run to make it 56-45 with 3:16 left.

"To beat that team, we've got to play perfect," said Kiffin, the former Alabama offensive coordinator. "We didn't do that. Obviously, we didn't play well on defense."

After another Ole Miss field goal, Alabama recovered an onside kick and Harris busted a 39-yard touchdown run moments later to seal it.

Alabama trailed 14-7 in the second quarter and then scored touchdowns on eight straight possessions on drives of 72, 75, 85, 52, 72, 44, 90 and 44 yards.

"We scored every time we had to score," Tide coach Nick Saban said. "We took the air out of it at the end of the game."

Kiffin worked for Saban at Alabama from 2014-16 and became the latest former Saban assistant to come up short against the old boss.

Saban improved to 21-0 against his former assistants, but he did suggest Kiffin and his staff might have been able to decipher the Tide's defensive signals.

"I definitely think so," said Alabama linebacker Dylan Moses, agreeing with his head coach.

Kiffin's offense made the Tide work hard. The Rebels got nearly 250 yards rushing and four touchdowns from Snoop Conner (128 yards) and Jerrion Ealy (120).

"We've never played this way on defense," Saban said. "It's certainly not what we try to aspire to be as a defensive team. I believe in our players. We have to get our players to play better. I think we're capable of it."

Emil Ekiyor Jr. lifts Najee Harris in celebration after Harris broke a Mississippi tackle and scored during the first half of Alabama's win over the Rebels in October.

AP PHOTO/ROGELIO V. SOLIS

Mississippi running back Jerrion Ealy is tackled by Alabama defenders in the second half of the Crimson Tide's 63-48 win.

AP PHOTO/ROGELIO V. SOLIS

Alabama quarterback Mac Jones passes while being pursued by Mississippi's Ryder Anderson.

AP PHOTO/ROGELIO V. SOLIS

Jaylen Waddle pulls in
a pass over Mississippi
defensive back A.J.
Finley.

AP PHOTO/ROGELIO V. SOLIS

Staying Power

Alabama's Nick Saban is Coach Killer of the SEC

AP PHOTO/RON JENKINS

ATLANTA — They keep trying to knock him off.

Occasionally, they're successful.

A Kick Six here. A Joe Burrow there.

In the end, though, no one in the Southeastern Conference comes close to Nick Saban.

He's the ultimate Coach Killer.

Over his 14-year reign at Alabama, the other 13 SEC schools have shuffled through a total of 35 coaches, who either were fired, quit, retired or moved on to other jobs.

More tellingly, those schools have doled out at least $120 million in buyouts to coaches who weren't up to the task — all in a futile quest to find someone, anyone, who can topple Saban.

Three more SEC coaches bit the dust this season, most notably Auburn's Gus Malzahn, who guided the Crimson Tide's fiercest rival to intermittent success against the Saban dynasty — but not enough to keep his job.

In the midst of a financially challenging pandemic, the Tigers will have to pay Malzahn more than $21 million to go away. That's on the top of settlements reached with their previous two coaches (Tommy Tuberville and Gene Chizik), which cost the school at least $12.5 million.

At 69 — the same age, by the way, that Bear Bryant retired as Alabama's coach — Saban shows no sign of slowing down.

"Obviously I love doing what I do, and want to continue to do it for as long as I feel like I can contribute in a positive way to the program," Saban said. "That's about the only plan I have for the future."

Why would he stop now?

This year's Alabama team might be his best yet, having breezed through a 10-game, SEC-only schedule with a perfect record. No game was closer than 15 points, the average margin of victory for the top-ranked Crimson Tide a whopping 32.7 points.

And if anyone needed a reminder of how this behemoth keeps regenerating year after year, even after sending countless first-round draft picks to the NFL, Saban landed what is projected to be the nation's top recruiting class during this week's early signing period.

"It's almost unfair," Steve Spurrier, the former Florida coach who once cast a nearly Saban-like presence over the SEC, told Sports Illustrated for a profile piece this week.

Alabama, he said, was "like being in the NFL, winning the Super Bowl and every year they get the first 10 picks in the first round. And then they get 10 in the second round and the rest of you guys take everyone else."

Saban's juggernaut heads into Saturday's SEC championship game in Atlanta as a whopping 17-point favorite over No. 11 Florida, not exactly a slouch of a team.

The Gators' coach, Dan Mullen, has faced the Tide nine times.

Nine times, he's lost.

At least he still has a job.

"I guess I've survived because I'm still here," quipped Mullen, who indeed has the second-longest coaching tenure in the SEC, having spent

Nick Saban speaks to CBS Sports before Alabama's faces LSU.

AP PHOTO/MATTHEW HINTON

nine years at Mississippi State (where all nine of those losses occurred) before moving to Florida — and out of Saban's division, if nothing else — in 2018.

Mullen sounds almost resigned to playing second-fiddle to the Crimson Tide as long as Saban is around.

"I don't know that it is knock them off or replace them. I don't know that they're going to go anywhere," Mullen said. "You just want to get up to their level and go compete on the same level as they are, and then go compete with them on a yearly basis."

There have been some one-year wonders.

Remember Auburn back in 2010? With Heisman Trophy winner Cam Newton at quarterback, the Tigers rallied from a 24-point deficit for a 28-27 victory in Tuscaloosa on their way to a national championship.

By 2012, the Tigers had plummeted to a winless mark in the SEC that culminated with a 49-0 blowout to Alabama. The day after that embarrassment, Chizik was fired.

Or how about LSU just last season? Led by the record-setting

Nick Saban leads the Crimson Tide onto the field
before the Rose Bowl.

AP PHOTO/RON JENKINS

Burrow, the Tigers knocked off Alabama in a 46-41 thriller, capped a perfect season by winning the national championship, and were touted as the nascent power in the SEC.

They had a charismatic coach in Ed Orgeron, who seemed the perfect fit to lock down a state rich in high school talent. They looked like the sort of program that could actually stand up to the big, bad Tide on a regular basis.

So much for that theory. When the teams met two weeks ago in Baton Rouge, Saban extracted his revenge with an ugly 55-17 beatdown. LSU will need to win Saturday's regular-season finale against Ole Miss just to salvage a 5-5 season.

All around the SEC, schools have tried futilely to uncover a coach who can stand up to Saban.

Will Muschamp has gotten a couple of opportunities, first at Florida, then at South Carolina. He was fired in both places, though the sting was surely offset by buyouts that will apparently total somewhere in the neighborhood of $20 million.

Not a bad neighborhood.

Georgia dumped longtime coach Mark Richt after the 2015 season and hired Saban protege Kirby Smart, who has guided the Bulldogs to a stellar record but is 0-3 against his former boss, including losses in the national championship game and the SEC title game.

Tennessee has already gone through four coaches in the Saban era and turned to another of his former assistants, Jeremy Pruitt, in hopes of being more competitive against the Tide.

But Pruitt is already on the hot seat after just three seasons, having lost every year to Alabama by an average margin of 30 points.

The famed "Third Saturday in October" rivalry has become a farce. The Volunteers have lost 14 straight games to the Crimson Tide, their last victory coming in 2006 — the year before Saban arrived.

SEC Commissioner Greg Sankey said the key to Saban's success is his adaptability.

At the beginning of his Alabama tenure, the Tide was run-oriented team that relied heavily on its defense. These days, they're a high-flying bunch averaging 49.5 points a game and led by two of the leading Heisman Trophy contenders, quarterback Mac Jones and receiver DeVonta Smith.

"You have to recognize he has adapted over time, the number of points he's scoring, looking back to his early days as more of a defensive-minded coach," Sankey said.

The commish is careful with his words. He can't appear to show favoritism to Saban's dynasty, but surely knows that other schools in the football-crazy conference are desperate to keep up.

"When you have sustained success, everybody wants to be at that level," Sankey said. "That creates competitive pressure."

But it doesn't really matter how many times those other schools flip coaches, or how many millions they squander in hopes of uncovering the next Saban.

Not as long as the real thing resides in Tuscaloosa.

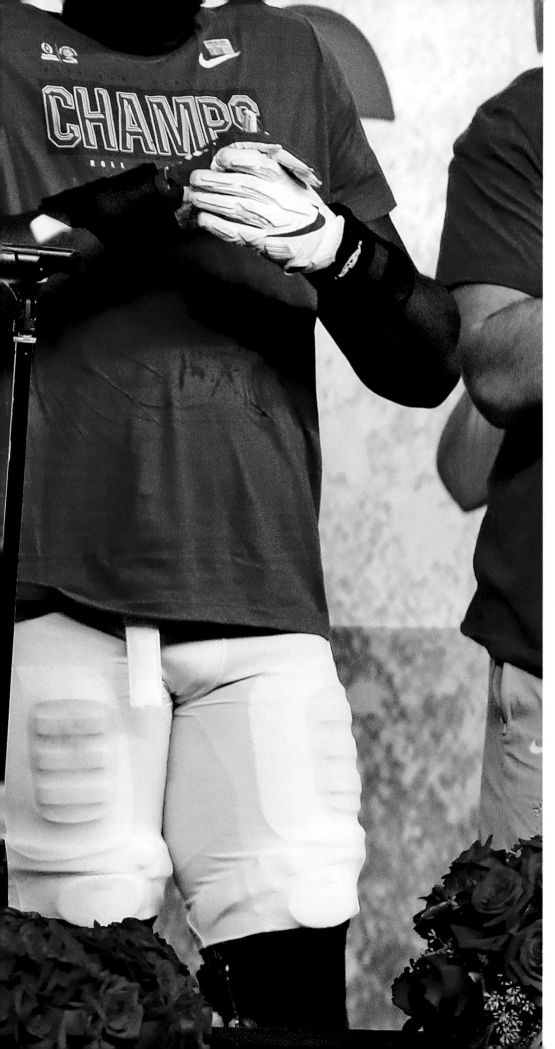

Nick Saban poses with the trophy after winning the Rose Bowl against Notre Dame.

AP PHOTO/ROGER STEINMAN

CRIMSON CRUSH

No. 2 Alabama roars back for 41-24 win over No. 3 Georgia

Oct 17, 2020

TUSCALOOSA, ALA. —A positive COVID-19 test couldn't keep Nick Saban from the sideline, and Georgia's heralded defense had scant hope of keeping Alabama's playmakers out of the end zone.

Mac Jones passed for 417 yards and four touchdowns and the No. 2 Crimson Tide picked apart No. 3 Georgia in the second half of a 41-24 victory Saturday night. It ended up being a decisive 'Bama victory in a collision of the Southeastern Conference's last remaining unbeaten teams.

The Crimson Tide (4-0), with Saban stalking the sideline after all, rallied with three touchdowns in a 10-minute span starting late in the third quarter.

The nation's top scoring offense ultimately got the emphatic upper hand in a battle with the Bulldogs (3-1) and one of the nation's best defenses.

"This was an obvious great win against a very, very good football team," said Saban, who was cleared early in the day after a false COVID positiv e. "I was very proud of the way our guys fought in the game.

"I sort of knew it was going to be a 15-round fight and we wouldn't be winning until the late rounds."

Georgia had no answer for Jones and star receivers Jaylen Waddle and DeVonta Smith, especially with Alabama's own beleaguered defense grabbing two second-half interceptions and three overall. Freshman Malachi Moore had one at the goal line and returned it 42 yards.

Smith caught 11 passes for 167 yards and two touchdowns, including one in the fourth quarter that effectively put it out of reach.

Waddle caught a 90-yard touchdown pass and gained 161 yards on six catches. Jones completed 24 of 32 passes and was strong after an interception on the opening play.

"The goal was just to win the game," Jones said. "You can look at their defense. They have good players in the secondary, they have good

linebackers, they have good defensive linemen but so do we."

Then there was some old-school ground and pound, too. Najee Harris gained 152 yards on 31 carries carries with a touchdown during that game-clinching span. He did it against the nation's top run defense, which came in allowing 38 rushing yards and 12.3 points per game.

Stetson Bennett completed 18 of 40 passes for 269 yards and two touchdowns, including an 82-yarder to James Cook. But he threw three interceptions.

Bennett was angry with himself over his mistakes, especially that final interception throwing across his body, calling it "just stupid."

"I was frustrated with myself," the former walk-on said.

Alabama got a boost about seven hours before the game when the SEC cleared coach Saban to return to business of usual, determining a Wednesday COVID test was a false positive. He tested negative Thursday, Friday and Saturday.

"That was very emotional," he said.

"It was very crazy," Jones said. "We were in our little quarterback meeting and he just showed up."

A maskless Saban was yelling at a referee after an intentional grounding call in the second quarter.

The Tide has won the last six meetings with Georgia, including a 3-0 record against Saban's former defensive coordinator, Kirby Smart. The first two came in the January 2018 national championship game and the SEC championship game the following season.

This was the first one that didn't go down to the wire. Georgia's defense allowed 564 yards.

"Just frustrated we couldn't get anything going in the second half, especially that opening drive," Smart said.

"I thought we were going to be able to run the ball and we stalled out and lost momentum after that point, especially after they hit the big long bomb to Waddle."

Devonta Smith makes a leaping catch for a touchdown in a 41-24 win over No. 3 Georgia at Bryant-Denney Stadium.

PHOTO BY UA ATHLETICS/ COLLEGIATE IMAGES/GETTY IMAGES

Najee Harris stiff-arms
a defender and outruns
the rest of the Georgia
defense in the first half.

*PHOTO BY UA ATHLETICS/
COLLEGIATE IMAGES/GETTY
IMAGES*

WIN IT FOR WADDLE

No. 2 Alabama loses Jaylen Waddle, beats Tennessee 48-17

Oct 24, 2020

KNOXVILLE, TENN. — Losing their most dynamic player left Alabama in no mood to celebrate - not even a big win over a longtime rival.

Wide receiver Jaylen Waddle broke his right ankle on the opening kickoff Saturday, about the only thing that didn't go the Crimson Tide's way in a 48-17 victory over Tennessee.

Mac Jones threw for 387 yards and ran for a touchdown, and Najee Harris ran for three more TDs as No. 2 Alabama added the 14th straight win in this rivalry.

The Crimson Tide (5-0) outgained Tennessee 587-302. But playing the Vols proved costly for Alabama a second straight season. A year ago, Tua Tagovailoa hurt an ankle in the second quarter and missed the next game against Arkansas.

On Saturday, Waddle rolled his right ankle as he was tackled on the opening kickoff and was taken by cart to the locker room. Waddle came out after catching the ball deep in the end zone, something coaches usually don't want. But Alabama coach Nick Saban said he trusts the judgment of the talented player.

Saban said Waddle has a similar injury to what Kenyan Drake had with a high ankle sprain with a fracture that probably will need surgery. Waddle will be flown back privately with doctors and taken to Birmingham to see if surgery is needed right away.

"If that's the case, and we're pretty certain that it is, he would probably be out for the year," Saban said.

Tennessee (2-3) forced Alabama to punt on its opening drive. That was as close as the Vols would get in losing their seventh straight in this series in Neyland Stadium. Coach Jeremy Pruitt, now 0-3 against his old boss, said he's obviously disappointed. Saban improved to 23-0 against his former assistants.

"I'm not used to this for sure, and I know the players in our locker room this isn't what they came here for either," Pruitt said. "These guys are hungry, they want to improve and they will because of that."

Jones got the Tide moving on the second drive, distributing the ball to different receivers on the first four plays. Harris appeared to fumble on his first carry on the drive but was ruled down before the ball came out, which was upheld on review. Harris scored on the next play.

Jones capped the next drive with a 1-yard plunge and a 14-0 lead. Alabama led 28-10 at halftime.

Harris added TD runs of 2 and 1 yards, and the senior running back finished with 96 yards on 20 carries. He also caught six passes for 61 more yards. Brian Robinson Jr. also had a 7-yard TD run.

Vols coach Jeremy Pruitt went for the 33-yard field goal by Brent Cimaglia on fourth-and-2 early in the second. Tennessee managed one TD drive in the first half with Jarrett Guarantano hitting freshman Jalin Hyatt on a 38-yard TD. Guarantano added a 27-yard TD pass to Josh Palmer to make it 42-17 late in the third.

Saban liked how his defense played.

"This is probably the best we've played, even though there's some plays in there that you could be critical of," Saban said. "But I was kind of proud of the way the guys played. They played with a little more confidence, and we were pretty aggressive."

Mac Jones lines up a pass against Tennessee on October 24.

CAITIE MCMEKIN/KNOXVILLE NEWS SENTINEL VIA AP

◄ Jaylen Waddle pushes away Tennessee defensive back Kenney Solomon. Waddle was injured in the game but the Tide cruised to a 48-17 win.

▼ Alabama defensive back Malachi Moore (13) celebrates a touchdown against the Vols.

PHOTOGRAPHS BY CAITIE MCMEKIN/KNOXVILLE NEWS SENTINEL VIA AP

Alabama running back Trey Sanders is tackled by Tennessee defensive back Tamarion McDonald during the fourth quarter.

CAITIE MCMEKIN/KNOXVILLE NEWS SENTINEL VIA AP

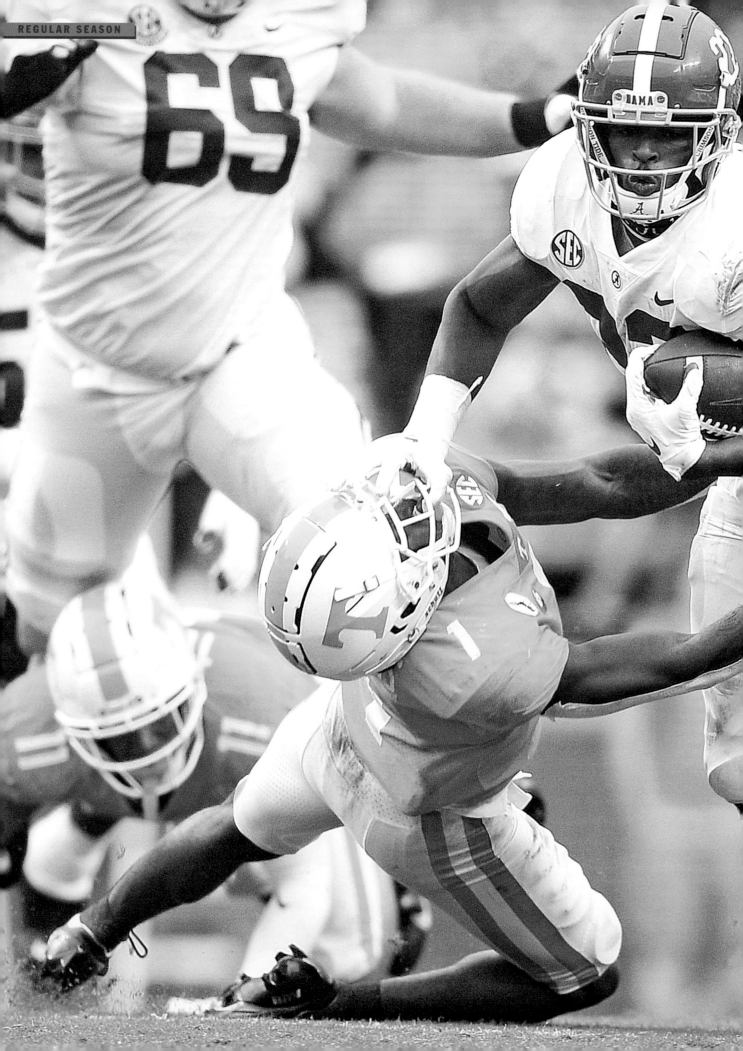

Najee Harris pushes back Tennessee defensive back Trevon Flowers in the second half. Harris scored three touchdowns in the decisive win.

CAITIE MCMEKIN/KNOXVILLE NEWS SENTINEL VIA AP

SHUTOUT

Smith, No. 2 Alabama pummel Mississippi State, 41-0

Oct 31, 2020

Tuscaloosa, Ala. — Alabama still has DeVonta Smith, another playmaking wide receiver who's awfully hard to defend. Mac Jones threw four touchdown passes to Smith and the wideout had 203 yards receiving as the second-ranked Crimson Tide began life without Jaylen Waddle with a 41-0 victory over Mississippi State on Saturday night without.

The Crimson Tide (6-0) had a dominant defensive performance, handing new Bulldogs coach Mike Leach the first shutout of his college career. It was Alabama's first shutout since a 24-0 victory over Mississippi State on Nov. 10, 2018.

"We did a lot of research in the offseason on who played them well and who played that offense well, even at Washington State," Tide coach Nick Saban said. They put "bits and pieces" of those approaches together and worked some on facing the offense in preseason camp, he said.

It worked well, and so did Alabama's short-handed offense.

Smith caught first-quarter touchdowns passes of 35 and 53 yards to help send the Bulldogs (1-4) to their fourth straight loss.

Smith took over the starring receiving role in the absence of Waddle, lost to a likely season-ending ankle injury. He made 11 catches and moved into a tie with Amari Cooper for the most career receiving touchdowns with No. 31 early in the fourth.

Smith also vaulted over Jerry Jeudy and Calvin Ridley into No. 3 on Alabama's career receiving yards list with 2,868.

"It's just a blessing to be in this position, just to be up there with the greats that came through and set the standard for me," said Smith, adding that he didn't feel any pressure without Waddle.

Jones completed 24 of 31 for 291 yards before sitting out most of the fourth. Najee Harris gained 119 yards on 21 carries.

Mississippi State quarterback K.J. Costello left after appearing to take a knee to the helmet early in the second quarter. He was escorted to the locker room and replaced by Will Rogers, who was coming off a 15-of-18 performance against Texas A&M.

Leach didn't disclose the nature of Costello's injury. He finished 4 of 11 for just 16 yards. Rogers completed 24 of 37 passes for 147 yards and threw two interceptions.

"I thought we played hard. I thought we played sloppy and dumb at times," Leach said. "I think that Alabama is a team that has been put together for over a decade. They have a culture that is extremely hard-working and competitive that permeates their entire program.

"We're a program that is trying to get there."

Alabama extended its major college record with a 19th straight game scoring at least 35 points, thanks to Patrick Surtain Jr.'s 25-yard pick-6 with 2:12 left.

Mississippi State mustered only one serious scoring threat but Dylan Moses intercepted a pass in the end zone late in the third.

"We planned on doing what we needed to do to stop the Air Raid attack," Surtain said. "I feel like carrying this momentum into the weeks ahead will give us a slight advantage."

Tight end Miller Forristall reaches up for a pass with Mississippi State safety Marcus Murphy defending during their matchup on Halloween. Murphy was called for pass interference on the play.

GARY COSBY JR./THE TUSCALOOSA NEWS VIA AP

Defensive back Patrick Surtain II makes an interception that he returned for a touchdown against Mississippi State during the second half.

GARY COSBY JR./THE TUSCALOOSA NEWS VIA AP

Wide receiver DeVonta Smith catches a touchdown pass in front of Mississippi State cornerback Emmanuel Forbes.

GARY COSBY JR./THE TUSCALOOSA NEWS VIA AP

CATCHING A RECORD

Smith, No. 1 Alabama rout short-handed Kentucky, 63-3

Nov 21, 2020

TUSCALOOSA, ALA. — Alabama didn't quite look like itself at first after an extended period on the sidelines, but it scarcely made a difference on the scoreboard.

DeVonta Smith caught nine passes for 144 yards and set the Southeastern Conference career record with two more touchdowns in the top-ranked Crimson Tide's 63-3 victory over short-handed Kentucky on Saturday.

"I think we played better and better and better as the game went on," coach Nick Saban said.

And the score got bigger and bigger and bigger.

Mac Jones passed for 230 yards and two touchdowns and Najee Harris ran for a pair of scores for the Tide (7-0 SEC), both in less than three quarters.

A slow start turned into a breezy return from a three-week layoff after LSU was forced to call off last week's scheduled game because of COVID-19 troubles.

The outmanned Wildcats (3-5) were missing a number of key players because of injuries or coronavirus protocol. They were competitive early on the stat sheet, but it didn't hold up particularly long on the scoreboard after they gave up three second-quarter touchdowns.

"I know you're going to look at the score and say, 'Man, there's not a lot of good things.' But there was," Kentucky coach Mark Stoops said. "Early in the game, I thought our guys were playing extremely hard, extremely physical."

Smith broke Amari Cooper's SEC and Alabama record with his 32nd touchdown catch, a 10-yarder from Jones in the second quarter. He added an 18-yarder from freshman backup Bryce Young.

"It's certainly a blessing to have my name with all the greats that came to the SEC and this school," Smith said.

Jones completed 16 of 24 passes but also was intercepted at the goal line in a rare mistake. Harris had a career-long 42-yard touchdown run and gained 83 yards on 13 carries.

Kentucky quarterback Terry Wilson passed for just 120 yards and was benched after throwing an interception that Jordan Battle returned 45 yards for a touchdown in the third quarter.

Joey Gatewood and Beau Allen couldn't get anything going, either. The Wildcats gained 121 yards in the first quarter and 60 the rest of the way.

Kentucky played without leading rusher Chris Rodriguez, guard Luke Fortner, tight ends Justin Rigg and Brenden Bates, and linebackers Jamin Davis and D'Eryk Jackson. The school didn't disclose reasons for each player's absence.

Alabama quarterback Mac Jones throws a touchdown pass to wide receiver John Metchie III against Kentucky. Jones threw for two touchdowns in the rout.

MICKEY WELSH/THE MONTGOMERY ADVERTISER VIA AP

◄ DeVonta Smith makes a catch against Kentucky defensive back Brandin Echols. Smith set the SEC record for touchdown catches in a career during the game,

▼ Linebacker Will Anderson Jr. pressures Kentucky quarterback Terry Wilson.

PHOTOGRAPHS BY MICKEY WELSH/THE MONTGOMERY ADVERTISER VIA AP

Defensive lineman Byron Young tackles Kentucky running back JuTahn McClain for a loss.

MICKEY WELSH/THE MONTGOMERY ADVERTISER VIA AP

Jase McClellan tries to fend off Kentucky defensive back Kelvin Joseph..

MICKEY WELSH/THE MONTGOMERY ADVERTISER VIA AP

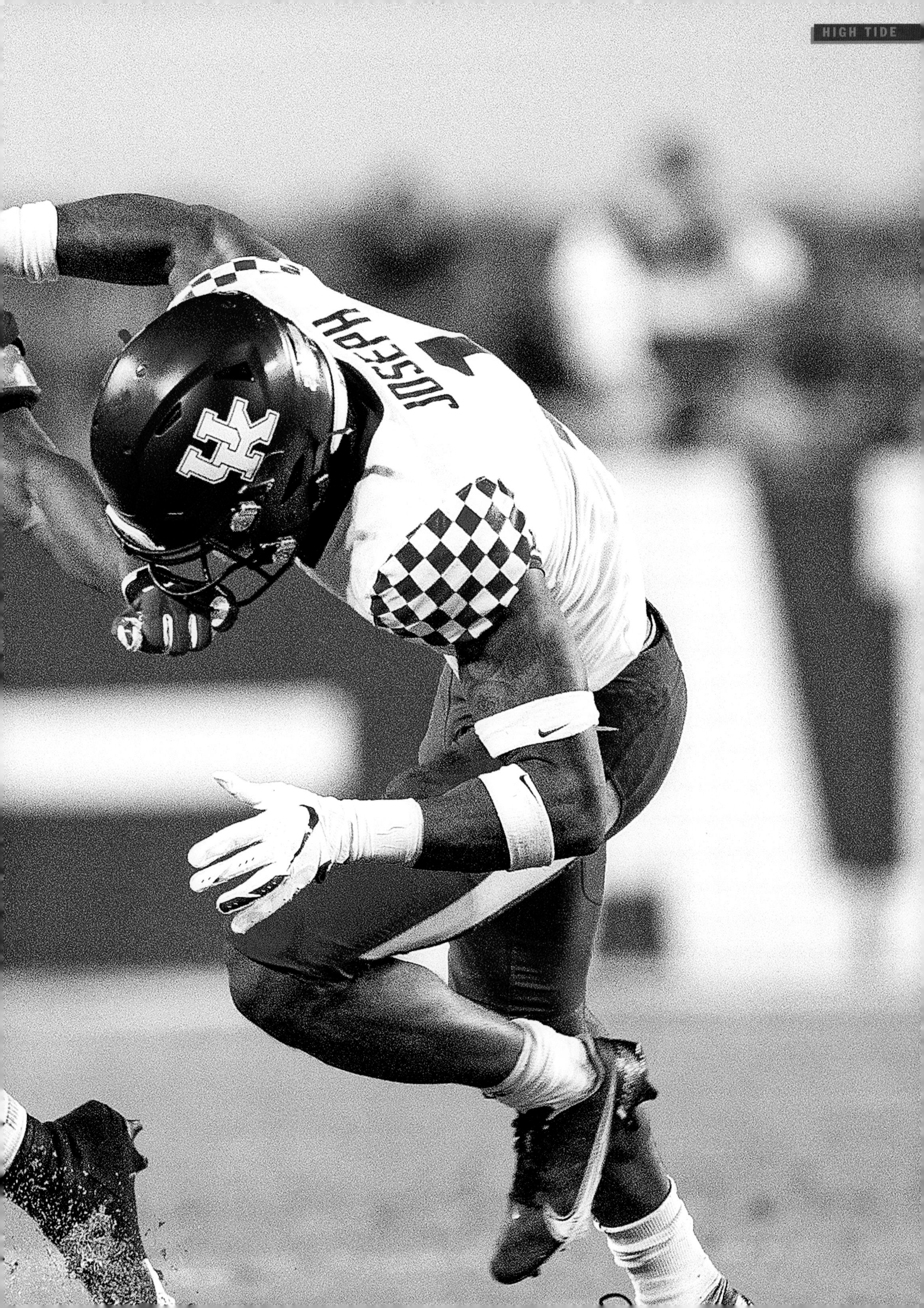
JOSEPH

IRON WILL

Jones, No. 1 Bama roll past No. 22 Auburn 42-13 minus Saban

Nov 28, 2020

TUSCALOOSA, ALA. — Once the Iron Bowl kicked off, Nick Saban was just another passionate, heavily invested fan who was powerless to help his team win.

His team still won — big .

Mac Jones passed for 302 yards and a career-high five touchdowns, highlighted by two long ones to DeVonta Smith, and No. 1 Alabama rolled over rival No. 22 Auburn 42-13 on Saturday without Saban.

The Crimson Tide (8-0, No. 1 playoff rankings) continued a dominating march through a schedule of all-Southeastern Conference games even minus its six-time national champion coach on the sideline.

Saban tested positive for COVID-19 on Wednesday and watched the game feed from home, witnessing the usual array of big plays with offensive coordinator Steve Sarkisian running the show.

Saban said his staff "did a marvelous job."

"Sark did a nice job of managing things, and I sat here and felt a little helpless," he said in a postgame zoom from his home. "I could see things and yell at things and listen to (wife) Miss Terry yell downstairs. It's a little different. It still feels good to win."

The result was much of the same against the Tigers (5-3), who suffered the second-most lopsided loss of Gus Malzahn's coaching tenure. The only bigger margin was Alabama's 52-21 win in the 2018 Iron Bowl.

"They're a very, very talented team," Malzahn said. "We knew that.

Still we came in here with the mindset that we wanted to win the game. To beat a team like that on the road, you've got to make plays. We didn't do that. We didn't play our best. It's obvious."

Alabama started a string of three straight touchdowns with Jones's 66-yard touchdown to Smith, who was streaking by himself downfield after Auburn defenders bit on a double move.

He later added a 58-yard catch and run on a quick slant, sprinting away from the Tigers.

Smith had seven catches for 171 yards. Najee Smith ran for 96 yards, including a 39-yard touchdown, and John Metchie III caught a pair of scoring passes.

"Not having Coach Saban is difficult and obviously he did a great job preparing all of us for a situation like this," Jones said. "It was clear we were prepared for this situation."

Bo Nix passed for 227 yards and ran for a late touchdown for the Tigers, but also threw two interceptions.

"It feels pretty terrible," Nix said. "It's not very fun. It just hurts because of everything that I've put into it, everything that I've done to get to this moment and just come up a lot short. It's an awful feeling, to be honest with you."

Saban, meanwhile, couldn't talk to his team starting 90 minutes before kickoff though he still led the preparation during the week. He spoke to the media in his home's "recruiting room," filled with Alabama memorabilia, including an elephant head on the wall and a pool table with a crimson playing surface.

"That was really hard, especially the fact that I feel great," the 69-year-old said.

Auburn defensive back Nehemiah Pritchett defends Alabama wide receiver John Metchie during the Iron Bowl.

MICKEY WELSH/THE MONTGOMERY ADVERTISER VIA AP

◀ DeVonta Smith and John Metchie III celebrate Smith's touchdown against Auburn.

▼ Smith (6) is put on his head by Auburn defensive lineman Derick Hall.

▼ A prerecorded message from coach Nick Saban is shown on the big screen at Bryant-Denny Stadium before the Iron Bowl on Nov. 28 in Tuscaloosa. Alabama won, 42-13.

PHOTOGRAPHS BY MICKEY WELSH/THE MONTGOMERY ADVERTISER VIA AP

◀ Tight end Jahleel Billingsley scores a touchdown against Auburn defensive back Jamien Sherwood.

▼ Auburn coach Gus Malzahn shouts from the sidelines.

PHOTOGRAPHS BY MICKEY WELSH/THE MONTGOMERY ADVERTISER VIA AP

Auburn receiver Anthony
Schwartz is tripped by
Alabama defensive back
Malachi Moore during the
Iron Bowl.

*MICKEY WELSH/THE
MONTGOMERY ADVERTISER
VIA AP*

Mac Jones carries the ball against Auburn.

MICKEY WELSH/THE MONTGOMERY ADVERTISER VIA AP

LOUISIANA COOKING

Jones bolsters Heisman case; No. 1 Alabama beats LSU 55-17

Dec 5, 2020

BATON ROUGE, LA. — Mac Jones passed for 385 yards and four touchdowns and No. 1 Alabama used a slew of explosive plays to run away from LSU 55-17 on Saturday night.

Jones threw three of his touchdown passes to Louisiana native DeVonta Smith, who went to the same high school as Louisiana Gov. John Bel Edwards and finished with eight catches for 231 yards in his return to his home state.

Smith's first two touchdowns went for 65 and 61 yards to cap three-play, 75-yard drives for Alabama (9-0, 9-0 SEC). But his third touchdown catch from 20-yards out appeared to be his most difficult. He shed close coverage from top LSU cornerback Derrick Stingley Jr. and made a twisting, leaping catch high over his head before landing on his back deep in the end zone.

Najee Harris rushed for 145 yards and three touchdowns on 21 carries, juking, shedding and even leaping over LSU defenders along the way.

LSU (3-5, 3-5) showed signs of life in the second quarter, scoring on a pair of long plays.

One nearly didn't happen when receiver Kayshon Bouttee caught a 43-yard pass and released the ball in celebration just before crossing the goal line. Luckily for LSU, Jontre Kirkland was following the play and picked the ball up in the end zone to complete LSU's first scoring play against Alabama in Tiger Stadium since 2014.

Later, John Emery Jr. ran for a 54-yard touchdown, the longest run allowed by Alabama this season. Each score pulled LSU as close as two touchdowns, but the Tide answered each with the two deep connections between Jones and Smith.

Jones had 338 yards and four TDs passing by halftime, when Smith had seven catches for 219 yards. Smith's third TD gave the Crimson Tide a 45-14 lead by halftime.

Alabama wasted little time breaking the game open.

Aided by an LSU offside penalty on third and 3, Alabama drove 75 yards in seven plays on the opening series, taking a 7-0 lead on Harris' zig-zagging, 14-yard run.

LSU responded by quickly driving to the Alabama 15, briefly enlivening the socially distanced crowd of 22,349 in 102,000-seat Death Valley, only to come up short on third and 1 and fourth and 1 — both rushes by Tyrion Davis-Price.

Two plays later, Alabama was inside LSU's 20 after Harris rushed for 28 yards down the left sideline and LSU was penalized 15 yards for a late hit out of bounds.

Soon after, Harris scored from a yard out to make it 14-0.

Before the first quarter ended, Jones connected with wide-open tight end Jahleel Billingsley on the left side of the field for a 24-yard score that made it 21-0.

That marked the most points allowed in a first quarter by LSU since coach Ed Orgeron took over four games into the 2016 season.

Tight end Jahleel
Billingsley scores during
the first half of a 55-17
win over LSU.

AP PHOTO/MATTHEW HINTON

Crimson Tide linebacker Ale Kaho celebrates a tackle for a loss against LSU in Baton Rouge, La., on Dec. 5.

AP PHOTO/MATTHEW HINTON

DeVonta Smith makes a touchdown grab against LSU cornerback Derek Stingley Jr. during the first half.

AP PHOTO/MATTHEW HINTON

DeVonta Smith runs after a catch against LSU during Alabama's blowout victory over the defending national champions.

AP PHOTO/MATTHEW HINTON

DeVonta Smith blows kisses to the stands after a touchdown during the first half.

AP PHOTO/MATTHEW HINTON

NEVER BETTER

Smith's TD return sparks No. 1 Tide's 52-3 rout of Arkansas

Dec 12, 2020

FAYETTEVILLE, ARK. — Alabama has been the dominant program in college football for more than a decade and Arkansas coach Sam Pittman has been coaching in the Southeastern Conference almost all of it.

After the top-ranked Crimson Tide buried Pittman's Razorbacks 52-3 on Saturday, the veteran coach said he believes the Crimson Tide has never been better.

"On tape, it's the best Alabama team I've seen," said Pittman, a longtime assistant at Tennessee, Arkansas and Georgia in his first season has head coach." (Alabama coach Nick Saban) is going to hate me for saying that. I think he calls that rat poison. But that's how I believe. That's the best squad I've seen. They're hard to stop."

DeVonta Smith returned a punt 84 yards for a touchdown as Alabama scored 28 points in a span of 11 minutes in the first half .

After the teams traded field goals, Smith started the Crimson Tide (10-0, CFP No. 1) barrage. Najee Harris scored consecutive touchdowns just 14 seconds apart and a final plunge from 1 yard by Brian Robinson Jr. had Alabama in cruising toward the Southeastern Conference championship game next week against No. 6 Florida.

"One of the motivating factors was win 10 SEC games in a regular season which has never been done before," Saban said. "And obviously we wanted to play to a standard. We got started a little slow and as the game went on, we got better and better on defense and controlled the tempo on offense. All in all, I was really pleased. We got to play a lot of players."

It was an otherwise quiet day for Smith, with three catches for 22 yards, but the receiver bolstered his surging case for Heisman Trophy consideration on one play.

"We gave up 76 yards early in the game, then we went for a good little stretch where they didn't get a first down and we started getting momentum on offense. The punt return was big," Saban said.

Crimson Tide defenders racked up eight sacks, the fifth of which resulted in a fumble by Arkansas quarterback Feliepe Franks which was recovered by DJ Dale at the Razorbacks 4. Harris scored on the next play.

Alabama allowed 188 yards and kept Arkansas (3-7) from registering a first down during a streak of seven straight possessions from the first quarter to the third.

"We were having trouble picking them up," Pittman said. "I had trouble picking them up when I was (offensive line coach) at Georgia with arguably the best line in football. We have to figure out how to move the pocket. Nobody can just sit back there against Alabama."

Harris and Robinson finished with a combined 100 yards rushing and five touchdowns on 27 carries. Jase McLellan added a final rushing down, an 80-yarder, with 1:51 left. Mac Jones, whose day was finished in the third quarter, threw for 208 yards on 24 of 29 passing for Alabama.

Franks was one of three Arkansas quarterbacks to take snaps, including back-up K.J. Jefferson, who left in the third quarter with an apparent leg injury, bringing Franks back into the game to finish. They combined to go 9 of 17 for 108 yards.

Alabama running back Jase McClellan scores on an 80-yard run against Arkansas during the second half of the Tide's 52-3 romp in December.

AP PHOTO/MICHAEL WOODS

◀ Arkansas quarterback Feleipe Franks is tackled for a loss by Will Anderson Jr.

▼ Alabama defensive lineman Phidarian Mathis celebrates after sacking Feleipe Franks

▼ Alabama defenders Stephon Wynn Jr. (90) and Shane Lee put pressure on Feleipe Franks and tackle him for a loss.

AP PHOTOGRAPHS/MICHAEL WOODS

DeVonta Smith returns a punt for a touchdown against Arkansas during the first half.

AP PHOTO/MICHAEL WOODS

Honored

AP All-SEC: No. 1 Alabama leads the way for top awards

Mac Jones warms up before playing Arkansas in December.
Jones was named first-team All-SEC, one of many honors this season.

AP PHOTO/MICHAEL WOODS

Dec 23, 2020

COLUMBIA, S.C. — No. 1 Alabama is on top of the Southeastern Conference again.

The SEC champions dominated all-SEC honors as voted on by a panel of members of The Associated Press.

Nick Saban was voted the league's coach of the year, receiver DeVonta Smith nabbed SEC offensive player of the year honors and cornerback Patrick Surtain II is the defensive player of the year.

The only individual award the experienced Crimson Tide didn't snag was newcomer of the year, which went to Auburn freshman runner Tank Bigsby.

Alabama led the SEC in scoring at almost 50 points a game, so it's no surprise five Crimson Tide players were named to the first-team offense. Quarterback Mac Jones, his top target in Smith and SEC leading rusher Najee Harris were voted to the team, along with center Landon Dickerson and tackle Alex Leatherwood.

Surtain, the talented junior, and defensive lineman Christian Barmore were on the defensive first team.

Florida's Kyle Pitts was the team's tight end and his teammate, receiver Kardius Toney, was named as the all-purpose player.

South Carolina 1,000-yard rusher Kevin Harris joined Najee Harris in the backfield.

Kentucky's Darian Kinnard, Tennessee's Trey Smith and Georgia's Ben Cleveland filled out the first-team offensive line.

Anders Carlson of Auburn was voted the first-team kicker.

On defense, the line featured Dayo Odeyingbo of Vanderbilt, Bobby Brown III of Texas A&M and Trajan Jeffcoat of Missouri.

The linebackers were Nick Bolton of Missouri, Grant Morgan of Arkansas and Monty Rice of Georgia.

The Bulldogs had Erik Stokes as cornerback and Richard LeCounte as safety. Jalen Catalon of Arkansas was the final member of the secondary.

Georgia's Jake Camarda was named the first-team punter.

Gators quarterback Kyle Trask, who led the country with 4,125 yards and 43 touchdowns, headed up the second-team offense.

THE 2020 AP ALL-SEC TEAM, as selected by a panel of 18 sports writers and sportscasters who regularly cover the league:
("u-" denotes unanimous selection)

FIRST TEAM

Pos.	Name, School	Ht/Wt.	Yr.	Hometown
Offense				
QB	Mac Jones, Alabama	6-3/214	RJr.	Jacksonville, Florida
RB	u-Najee Harris, Alabama,	6-2/230	Sr.	Antioch, California
RB	Kevin Harris, South Carolina	5-10/225	So.	Hinesville, Georgia
T	u-Alex Leatherwood, Alabama	6-6/312	Sr.	Pensacola, Florida
T	Darian Kinnard, Kentucky	6-5/345	Jr.	Knoxville, Tennessee
C	Landon Dickerson, Alabama	6-6/325	RSr.	Hickory, North Carolina
G	Trey Smith, Tennessee	6-6/330	Sr.	Jackson, Tennessee
G	Ben Cleveland, Georgia	6-6/335	Sr.	Taccoa, Georgia
TE	u-Kyle Pitts, Florida	6-4/225	Jr.	Philadelphia
WR	u-DeVonta Smith, Alabama	6-1/175	Sr.	Amite, Louisiana
WR	Elijah Moore, Mississippi	5-9/184	Jr.	Fort Lauderdale, Florida
All-Purpose	Kadarius Toney, Florida	5-11/194	Sr.	Mobile, Alabama
K	Anders Carlsen, Auburn	6-5/215	Jr.	Colorado Springs, Colorado
Defense				
DE	Dayo Odeyingbo, Vanderbilt	6-6/276	Sr.,	Irving, Texas
DE	Trajan Jeffcoat, Missouri	6-3/265	RSo.	Irmo, South Carolina
DT	Christian Barmore, Alabama	6-5/310	RSo.	Philadelphia
DT	Bobby Brown III, Texas A&M	6-4/325	Jr.	Arlington, Texas
LB	Nick Bolton, Missouri	6-2/232	Jr.	Frisco, Texas
LB	Grant Morgan, Arkansas	5-11/222	RSr.	Greenwood, Arkansas
LB	Monty Rice, Georgia	6-1/235	Sr.	Huntsville, Alabama
CB	Patrick Surtain II, Alabama	6-2/202	Jr.	Plantation, Florida
CB	Erik Stokes, Georgia	6-1/185	Jr.	Covington, Georgia
S	Richard LeCounte, Georgia	5-11/190	Sr.,	Riceboro, Georgia
S	Jalen Catalon, Arkansas	5-10/189	RFr.	Mansfield, Texas
P	Jake Camarda, Georgia	6-2/180	Jr.	Norcross, Georgia

SECOND TEAM

Pos.	Name, School	Ht/Wt.	Yr.	Hometown
Offense				
QB	Kyle Trask, Florida	6-5/240	Sr.	Manvel, Texas
RB	Isaiah Spiller, Texas A&M	6-1/225	So.	Spring, Texas
RB	Tank Bigsby, Auburn	6-0/204	Fr.,	LaGrange, Georgia
T	Landon Young, Kentucky	6-7/321	Sr.	Lexington, Kentucky
T	Carson Green, Texas A&M	6-6/320	Sr.	Southlake, Texas
G	Kenyon Green, Texas A&M	6-4/325	So.	Humble, Texas
G	Deonte Brown, Alabama	6-4/350	RSr.	Decatur, Alabama
C	Drake Jackson, Kentucky	6-2/292	Sr.	Versailles, Kentucky
TE	Jalen Wydermyer, Texas A&M	6-5/265	So.	Dickinson, Texas
WR	Treylon Burks, Arkansas	6-3/232	So.	Warren, Arkansas
WR	Kadarius Toney, Florida	5-11/194	Sr.	Mobile, Alabama
All-Purpose	Jerrion Ealy, Mississippi	5-8/190	So.	Walnut Grove, Mississippi
K	Cade York, LSU	6-1/198	So.	McKinney, Texas
Defense				
DE	Ali Gaye, LSU	6-6/262	Jr.	Lynnwood, Washington
DE	Brenton Cox Jr., Florida	6-4/249	Jr.	Lithonia, Georgia
DT	Kingsley Enagbare, South Carolina	6-4/270	Jr.	Atlanta
DT	Jonathan Marshall, Arkansas	6-3/317	RSr.	Shepherd, Texas
LB	Azeez Ojulari, Georgia	6-3/240	RSo.	Marietta, Georgia
LB	Willie Anderson Jr., Alabama	6-4/235	Fr.	Hampton, Georgia
LB	Henry To'o To'o, Tennessee	6-2/225	So.	Sacramento, California
CB	Kaiir Elam, Florida	6-2/194	So.	Riviera Beach, Florida
CB	Eli Ricks, LSU	6-2/196	Fr.	Rancho Cucamonga, California
S	Smoke Munday, Auburn	6-2/196	Jr.	Atlanta
S	Malachi Moore, Alabama	6-0/182	Fr.	Trussville, Alabama
P	Max Duffy, Kentucky	6-1, 190	Sr.	Perth, Australia

Coach of the year — Nick Saban, Alabama. | Offensive player of the year — DeVonta Smith, WR, Alabama | Defensive player of the year — Patrick Surtain II, CB, Alabama | Newcomer of the year — Tank Bigsby, RB, Auburn.

Najee Harris on a long
run against Auburn in the
Iron Bowl.

*MICKEY WELSH/THE
MONTGOMERY ADVERTISER
VIA AP*

FIRST TEST

Harris scores 5 TDs, No. 1 Bama escapes No. 11 Florida 52-46

Dec 19, 2020

ATLANTA – In a season of blowouts, Alabama finally got tested. Against a team that just wouldn't quit, the Crimson Tide required every last point.

Nick Saban needed his offensive stars to shine as bright as they have all season.

Boy, did they ever.

Najee Harris rushed for 178 yards and scored five touchdowns. Mac Jones threw for 418 yards and five TDs. DeVonta Smith hauled in 15 receptions for 184 yards and two scores.

It was just enough to send No. 1 Alabama to the College Football Playoff with a perfect record, holding off No. 11 Florida in a 52-46 shootout for the Southeastern Conference championship Saturday night.

"Those guys are pretty phenomenal. They have been all year," Saban said. "They certainly delivered tonight when we needed them to."

The Crimson Tide (11-0, No. 1 CFP) got its toughest challenge in a season of blowouts, but the result was the same. Another win. Now, with one of his best teams yet, the 69-year-old coach heads to the playoff in search of his seventh national title.

"This has been a year with a lot of disruptions," said Saban, who had his own bout with COVID-19. "The resiliency this team has shown this season to win 11 games is pretty phenomenal."

After trailing 35-17 at halftime, Florida (8-3, No. 7 CFP) made a game of it with a pair of third-quarter scores. And the Gators fought to the bitter end, adding two more TDs in the fourth period before the clock hit zero.

"We were rolling pretty good," said quarterback Kyle Trask, who threw for 408 yards and three TDs. "We just ran out of time."

Harris, the game's MVP, essentially established residency in the Mercedes-Benz Stadium end zones.

The senior running back had 31 bruising carries, scoring on plays of 8 and 1 yards and leaping like a hurdler over a defender who tried to go low on a 19-yard run.

Amazingly, Harris was even more dynamic in the passing game. He hauled in five throws for 67 yards, including touchdown plays of 23, 17 and 7 yards in Alabama's first-half blitz.

The shortest of those scoring catches may have been his best, as Harris sent a would-be tackler tumbling to the turf with a dazzling spin move.

"I've been catching the ball since birth," he quipped. "People don't expect it because of the running back name, but I can catch."

Harris set an SEC championship game record with his five touchdowns, breaking the mark of four scored by Auburn's Tre Mason in 2013. The Alabama senior also knocked off a couple of school records, setting new standards for career rushing TDs (44) and overall TDs (54).

The two quarterbacks did nothing to hurt their standing as two of the leading Heisman Trophy contenders. Neither did Smith, the Crimson Tide's other top candidate.

Mac Jones throws during the SEC Championship win over Florida on December 19 in Atlanta.

PHOTO BY DAVID J. GRIFFIN/ICON SPORTSWIRE VIA AP IMAGES

Alabama running back Najee Harris celebrates one of his five touchdowns against Florida in the SEC Championship.

AP PHOTO/JOHN BAZEMORE

After Saturday night's performance, Harris should probably be in the mix as well.

"I'm not worried about that," he said. "The two guys we've got up there now is good enough."

In addition to catching all those passes, Smith came up with a key fumble recovery after Florida's Trey Dean picked off a throw from Jones, snatching the ball away from the intended receiver, only to cough it up on a brutal, blind-side hit by Alabama receiver John Metchie.

Jones threw a 31-yard touchdown pass to Smith on the very next play.

Trask was 26 of 40 with a 51-yard scoring pass early on to Kadarius Toney, who finished with eight receptions for 153 yards. The Gators quarterback also hooked up with Trevon Grimes on a 50-yard touchdown throw, in addition to scoring one of his own with a 1-yard run.

Give Florida credit: Coming off a shocking home loss to LSU, the Gators fought to the very end.

"I thought we showed a lot of character," coach Dan Mullen said. "That was an excellent team we played ... give them credit. That's why they're ranked No. 1 in the country."

The final quarter was thriller for the socially distanced crowd of 16,520 scattered throughout the 75,000-seat stadium.

After Harris' lunged over from the 1 for final TD to extend Alabama's lead to 45-31, the Gators responded with a nine-play, 75-yard scoring drive that culminated with Damien Pierce's own 1-yard touchdown plunge.

Alabama's high-powered offense struck right back. Harris ripped off a 29-yard run deep into Florida territory, and Smith finished it off by hauling in a 15-yard scoring pass from Jones after a play-action fake to Harris froze the Gators defense.

Florida had one more big drive in its arsenal, zipping down the field on another 75-yard possession that ended with Trask lofting a 22-yard TD pass to his star tight end, Kyle Pitts. Trask then ran for a two-point conversion.

That would be the last gasp.

Alabama recovered an onside kick and ran out all but the final 16 seconds. Trask was sacked on the final play of the game.

After missing the College Football Playoff a year ago for the first time since the four-team format was adopted in 2014, the Crimson Tide is back in familiar territory with an offense that averages nearly 50 points a game and seemingly has too many weapons for just 11 men to stop.

"I really love this team," Saban said.

Najee Harris scores
a first-half touchdown
against Florida.

AP PHOTO/BRYNN ANDERSON

Alabama defensive lineman Phidarian Mathis (48) celebrates with teammates after the Crimson Tide won the SEC Championship with a 52-46 win over Florida.
AP PHOTO/BRYNN ANDERSON

Alabama receiver Slade Bolden celebrates a Najee Harris touchdown in the first half.

AP PHOTO/JOHN BAZEMORE

Najee Harris (left) and offensive lineman Alex Leatherwood lift the SEC Championship trophy after defeating Florida.

AP PHOTO/BRYNN ANDERSON

Well Received

Alabama's Smith becomes 1st WR to win Heisman in 29 years

DeVonta Smith Mac Jones (10) celebrate a touchdown pass during the second half against Mississippi State on Halloween.

GARY COSBY JR./THE TUSCALOOSA NEWS VIA AP, FILE

Jan 5, 2021

NEW YORK — On an Alabama team stacked with stars, DeVonta Smith emerged as the best player in college football. Smith became the first wide receiver to win the Heisman Trophy in 29 seasons Tuesday night, breaking the monopoly quarterbacks have had on college football's most prestigious award by beating out three of them.

"I want to thank my teammates," Smith said during his acceptance speech. "With team success comes individual success so without you all, I wouldn't be where I'm at today, winning this award."

Smith finished with 447 first-place votes and 1,856 points to easily outdistance Clemson's Trevor Lawrence (222, 1,187), Alabama teammate Mac Jones (138, 1,130) and Florida's Kyle Trask (61, 737).

Crimson Tide running back Najee Harris finished fifth in the voting, making No. 1 Alabama the second team in the 95-year history of the Heisman to have three of the top five vote-getters. Army did it in 1946 with Glenn Davis (first), Doc Blanchard (fourth) and Arnold Tucker (fifth).

Smith, a senior, is the fourth receiver to win the Heisman, joining Michigan's Desmond Howard in 1991, Notre Dame's Tim Brown in 1987 and Nebraska's Johnny Rodgers in 1972.

Quarterbacks had won 17 of the previous 20 Heisman trophies, including the last four.

Smith was presented with the award in a virtual ceremony orchestrated by ESPN. The usual trip to New York for the finalists was called off because of the pandemic and the winner was announced later than it had ever been before.

Smith accepted the trophy in Tuscaloosa, Alabama, decked out in a deep crimson jacket and shiny black bow tie.

Meanwhile, his parents watched from a community center in his hometown of Amite, Louisiana, where a socially distanced watch party was held.

Smith is the third Alabama player to win the Heisman, all since 2009. Like Tide running backs Mark Ingram ('09) and Derrick Henry (2015), Smith will play in the national championship game as a Heisman winner.

The Heisman voting was complete on Dec. 21, so playoff performances were not a factor. But Smith made those who supported him feel good about it with a brilliant three-touchdown game against Notre Dame in the CFP semifinals last weekend.

Smith has 105 catches for 1,641 yards and 22 total touchdowns going into the final game of his college career — which will also be his third national championship game.

Smith carved out a place in Alabama's storied history as a freshman, catching the winning 41-yard touchdown pass from Tua Tagovailoa on second-and-26 in overtime against Georgia to give the Tide the 2017 national championship.

For the next two seasons, Smith was still often the overlooked star in

DeVonta Smith with the Heisman Trophy after being named the winner.
KENT GIDNEY/HEISMAN TROPHY TRUST VIA AP

Alabama wide receiver DeVonta Smith poses with the Heisman Trophy on January 5. Smith won the award with 447 first-place votes and 1,856 points to easily outdistance Clemson's Trevor Lawrence (222, 1,187), Alabama teammate Mac Jones (138, 1,130) and Florida's Kyle Trask (61, 737).

KENT GIDNEY/HEISMAN TROPHY TRUST VIA AP

the Tide's talented 2017 class of receivers that included All-American Jerry Jeudy and Henry Ruggs. Both of those players decided to skip their senior seasons and enter the draft last year. Both were selected in the first round.

Smith returned to school to complete his degree and form an explosive combination for the Tide with junior Jaylen Waddle. Then Waddle went down with a season-ending leg injury on Oct. 24.

As the Tide's undisputed No. 1 receiver, Smith shined. The week after Waddle went out, Smith had 11 catches for 204 yards and four touchdowns against Mississippi State.

Smith's soaring one-handed TD grab against LSU was not just his signature play, but one the 2020 season's best.

A former four-star recruit, Smith came to Tuscaloosa from LSU's backyard, disappointing the many Tigers' fans in his hometown.

He had only seven receptions as a freshman, and while he scored the winning touchdown in the national title game, the story was of the game was the guy who threw it.

Tagovailoa was Alabama's Heisman contender for the next two years.

The understated Smith quietly led the Tide in receptions and yards last year as a junior and became a second-team All-American.

Smitty — as teammates and coaches call him — didn't emerge as a Hesiman contender this season until Waddle went down.

Starting with that Mississippi State game, Smith went on a four-game tear with 35 catches for 749 yards and 11 touchdowns that solidified another nickname for the 6-foot-1, 175-pound technician: the Slim Reaper.

Whatever you want to call Smith, he's been quite a catch for Alabama.

DeVonta Smith hauls in a catch for a touchdown as Notre Dame cornerback Nick McCloud defends in the second half of the Rose Bowl.

AP PHOTO/MICHAEL AINSWORTH

ROLL THE ROSE BOWL

Roll Tide! No. 1 Alabama beats Notre Dame 31-14 in Rose Bowl

Jan 1, 2021

ARLINGTON, TEXAS – - A truly untraditional Rose Bowl setting, a very common result for Alabama in the College Football Playoff.

With Heisman Trophy finalists DeVonta Smith and Mac Jones, the top-ranked Crimson Tide rolled into its fifth CFP championship game in six seasons.

Smith caught three of Jones' four touchdown passes and Najee Harris ran for 125 yards with a high-hurdling highlight in a 31-14 victory over No. 4 Notre Dame in a CFP semifinal Rose Bowl played inside about 1,400 miles from Pasadena, California.

"I don't think there's anything quite like the Rose Bowl, the tradition, the setting, the mountains. It's just a phenomenal experience," coach Nick Saban said. "Wish our players had gotten that opportunity."

But Saban and the Tide (12-0, No. 1 CFP) will take yet another win in the home of the NFL's Dallas Cowboys, which the coach called one of college football's finest venues, and advancing again in the playoff.

The Tide earned a spot in the Jan. 11 championship game in suburban Miami, against No. 3 Ohio State, which beat Clemson 49-28 in the other CFP semifinal at the Sugar Bowl on Friday night.

Alabama missed the CFP last year for the only time since the four-time playoff debuted at the end of the 2014 season. The Buckeyes were the initial CFP champions, after beating the top-seeded Tide 42-35 in a semifinal that year.

Notre Dame (10-2, No. 4 CFP), in football's final four for only the second time, has lost seven consecutive New Year's Six games since 2000.

Alabama scored TDs on its first three possessions, including an 97-yard drive on which Harris leaped over 6-foot cornerback Nick McCloud just after crossing the line of scrimmage, landed on both feet and then sprinted for a 53-yard gain before getting run out of bounds.

"I don't know why I'm surprised every time he does it. I've seen it for three years, but still, 'Geez!," tight end Miller Forristall said.

"I actually try to teach him not to do it, and it didn't work," Saban said, laughing. "Anyway, for a big guy, it's pretty amazing that he can do that. He's kind of got a great feel when a guy's going to try to cut him. ... When he sees that head go down, he'll go over the top of them in a heartbeat."

Jones, who completed 25 of 30 passes for 297 yards, threw a 12-yard TD to tight end Jahleel Billingsley on the next play.

That came between drives when Smith, with 16 TD catches his last seven games, turned short passes into scores of 26 and 34 yards. Smith

DeVonta Smith runs during the Rose Bowl win over Notre Dame on January 1 in Arlington, Texas.

COOPER NEILL VIA AP

Najee Harris fights off a tackle by Notre Dame linebacker Drew White in the second half of Alabama's 31-14 Rose Bowl victory.

AP PHOTO/MICHAEL AINSWORTH

finished with seven catches for 130 yards, later adding a nifty toe-tapping 7-yarder in the front corner of the end zone right on the pylon.

CFP officials moved the Rose Bowl because of COVID-19 restrictions in California that would have kept family - or any fans - from attending the game at its normal home. There was a limited capacity crowd of 18,373 at AT&T Stadium, the home of the Dallas Cowboys, just a bit higher than attendance for the Cotton Bowl game there two nights earlier when Oklahoma beat SEC runner-up Florida 55-20.

It was another thud of a finish for the Fighting Irish after winning all 10 regular-season games, including a home victory over Clemson. But Notre Dame then lost 34-10 in the ACC title game to the Tigers.

"Today was about making the plays. They made them on the perimeter. Their skill players showed up today as they have all year," Irish coach Brian Kelly said. "We battled. I thought we did some of the things that we wanted to today but we simply didn't make enough plays."

Notre Dame lost 30-3 to Clemson in the CFP semifinal Cotton Bowl two years ago at AT&T Stadium. It was the first time the Irish had played Alabama since the Tide beat them 42-14 in the BCS national championship game eight seasons ago.

The Alabama defense kept quarterback Ian Book scrambling. The winningest starting QB ever for the Irish at 30-5, Book completed 27 of 39 passes for 229 yards and only his third interception in 353 attempts this season.

Crimson Tide linebacker Christian Harris makes an interception during the College Football Playoff Semifinal win over Notre Dame.

PHOTO BY GEORGE WALKER/ICON SPORTSWIRE VIA AP IMAGES

◀ DeVonta Smith runs after a catch for a 34 yard touchdown against Notre Dame.

JAMES D. SMITH VIA AP

▼ Alabama offensive lineman Javion Cohen holds a rose between his teeth after a 31-14 win over the Fighting Irish.

AP PHOTO/MICHAEL AINSWORTH

▼ Alabama fans cheer during the Rose Bowl victory over Notre Dame that sent the Crimson Tide to the National Championship game.

PHOTO BY MATTHEW PEARCE/ICON SPORTSWIRE VIA AP IMAGES

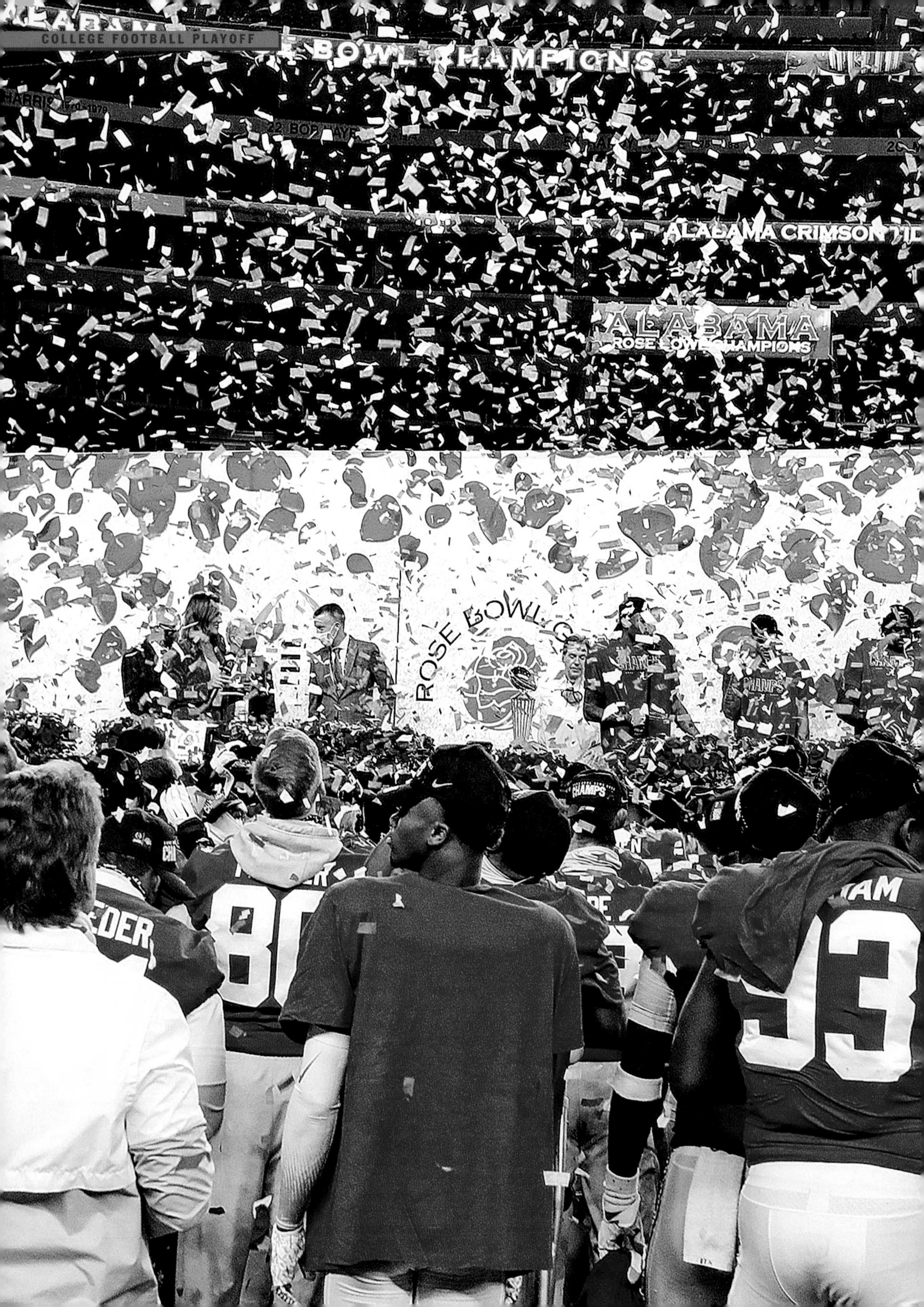
BOWL CHAMPIONS
ALABAMA CRIMSON TID
ALABAMA
ROSE BOWL

Confetti falls on the Alabama team after the Rose Bowl game on January 1 in Arlington at Cowboys Stadium. The Rose Bowl was played in Arlington because of California COVID-19 protocols. Alabama won and secured a place in the College Football Playoff championship.

JAMES D. SMITH VIA AP

TEAM ROSTER

2020 ALABAMA CRIMSON TIDE

	Name	Pos.	Ht.	Wt.	Year	Hometown/H.S. Last School
1	Ben Davis	LB	6-4	250	R-Sr.	Gordo, Ala. / Gordo
2	Keilan Robinson	RB	5-9	190	So.	Washington, D.C. / St. John's
2	Patrick Surtain II	DB	6-2	202	Jr.	Plantation, Fla. / American Heritage
3	Xavier Williams	WR	6-1	190	R-So.	Hollywood, Fla. / Chaminade-Madonna Prep
3	Daniel Wright	DB	6-1	195	R-Jr.	Fort Lauderdale, Fla. / Boyd Anderson
4	Christopher Allen	LB	6-4	250	Sr.	Baton Rouge, La. / Southern Lab School
4	Brian Robinson Jr.	RB	6-1	228	Sr.	Tuscaloosa, Ala. / Hillcrest
5	Jalyn Armour-Davis	DB	6-1	192	So.	Mobile, Ala. / St. Paul's
5	Javon Baker	WR	6-2	195	Fr.	Powder Springs, Ga. / McEachern
6	DeVonta Smith	WR	6-1	175	Sr.	Amite, La. / Amite
7	Braxton Barker	QB	6-1	202	R-So.	Birmingham, Ala. / Spain Park
7	Brandon Turnage	DB	6-1	186	R-Fr.	Oxford, Miss. / Lafayette
8	Christian Harris	LB	6-2	232	So.	Baton Rouge, La. / University Lab
8	John Metchie III	WR	6-0	195	So.	Brampton, Canada / St. James School (Md.)
9	Jordan Battle	DB	6-1	210	So.	Fort Lauderdale, Fla. / St. Thomas Aquinas
9	Bryce Young	QB	6-0	194	Fr.	Pasadena, Calif. / Mater Dei
10	Mac Jones	QB	6-3	214	R-Jr.	Jacksonville, Fla. / The Bolles School
10	Ale Kaho	LB	6-1	235	Jr.	Reno, Nev. / Reno
11	Traeshon Holden	WR	6-3	208	Fr.	Kissimmee, Fla. / Narbonne
11	Kristian Story	DB	6-1	215	Fr.	Lanett, Ala. / Lanett
12	Logan Burnett	QB	6-2	200	Sr.	Pelham, Ala. /Bessemer TCU/Mississippi St.
12	Skyler DeLong	P	6-4	188	Jr.	Fort Mill, S.C. / Nation Ford
13	Malachi Moore	DB	6-0	182	Fr.	Trussville, Ala. / Hewitt-Trussville
14	Brian Branch	DB	6-0	190	Fr.	Tyrone, Ga. / Sandy Creek
14	Thaiu Jones-Bell	WR	6-0	190	Fr.	Hallandale, Fla. / Miami Carol City
15	Eddie Smith	DB	6-0	196	R-So.	Slidell, La. / Salmen
15	Paul Tyson	QB	6-5	228	R-Fr.	Trussville, Ala. / Hewitt-Trussville
16	Jayden George	QB	6-3	192	Fr.	Indianapolis, Ind. / Warren Central
16	Will Reichard	PK	6-1	190	So.	Hoover, Ala. / Hoover
17	Jaylen Waddle	WR	5-10	182	Jr.	Houston, Texas / Episcopal
18	Slade Bolden	WR	5-11	191	R-So.	West Monroe, La. / West Monroe
18	LaBryan Ray	DL	6-5	295	R-Jr.	Madison, Ala. / James Clemens
19	Jahleel Billingsley	TE	6-4	230	So.	Chicago, Ill. / Phillips Academy
19	Stone Hollenbach	QB	6-3	208	R-Fr.	Catawissa, Pa. / Southern Columbia
20	Drew Sanders	LB	6-5	230	Fr.	Denton, Texas / Ryan
21	Jase McClellan	RB	5-11	212	Fr.	Aledo, Texas / Aledo
21	Jahquez Robinson	DB	6-2	190	Fr.	Jacksonville, Fla. / Sandalwood
22	Najee Harris	RB	6-2	230	Sr.	Antioch, Calif. / Antioch
22	Ronald Williams Jr.	DB	6-2	190	Jr.	Ferriday, La. / Ferriday Hutchinson C.C.
23	Jarez Parks	LB	6-4	240	R-So.	Fellsmere, Fla. / Sebastian River
23	Roydell Williams	RB	5-10	210	Fr.	Hueytown, Ala. / Hueytown
24	Clark Griffin	LB	5-9	195	Fr.	Mountain Brook, Ala. / Mountain Brook
24	Trey Sanders	RB	6-0	214	R-Fr.	Port Saint Joe, Fla. / IMG Academy
25	Jonathan Bennett	WR	5-8	178	Fr.	Birmingham, Ala. / Oak Mountain
25	DJ Douglas	DB	6-0	202	R-Fr.	Montgomery, Ala. / Thompson
25	Jacobi McBride	DB	6-1	143	Fr.	Madison, Ala. / Madison Academy
26	Marcus Banks	DB	6-0	180	So.	Houston, Texas / Dekaney
27	Kyle Edwards	RB	6-0	209	Fr.	Destrehan, La. / Destrehan
27	Joshua Robinson	DB	5-9	180	R-Jr.	Hoover, Ala. / Hoover
28	Josh Jobe	DB	6-1	192	Jr.	Miami, Fla. / Cheshire Academy (Conn.)
29	DeMarcco Hellams	DB	6-1	208	So.	Washington, D.C. / DeMatha Catholic
30	King Mwikuta	LB	6-5	238	So.	West Point, Ga. / Troup County
31	Will Anderson Jr.	LB	6-4	235	Fr.	Hampton, Ga. / Dutchtown
31	Shatarius Williams	WR	6-3	187	Fr.	Demopolis, Ala. / Demopolis
32	Dylan Moses	LB	6-3	240	Sr.	Alexandria, La. / IMG Academy
32	C.J. Williams	WR	5-10	159	Fr.	Gallion, Ala. / Demopolis
33	Jackson Bratton	LB	6-3	225	Fr.	Muscle Shoals, Ala. / Muscle Shoals
34	Quandarrius Robinson	LB	6-5	220	Fr.	Birmingham, Ala. / Jackson-Olin
35	Cooper Bishop	RB	6-0	195	R-Fr.	Vestavia Hills, Ala. / Vestavia Hills
35	Shane Lee	LB	6-0	240	So.	Burtonsville, Md. / St. Frances Academy
36	Bret Bolin	WR	6-0	176	R-Jr.	Lemont, Ill. / Lemont Indiana
37	Demouy Kennedy	LB	6-3	215	Fr.	Theodore, Ala. / Theodore
37	Sam Willoughby	DB	5-10	165	Fr.	Vestavia Hills, Ala. / Vestavia Hills
38	Jalen Edwards	DB	6-0	177	R-Fr.	Columbus, Miss. / Eufaula
39	Carson Ware	DB	6-1	190	R-Fr.	Muscle Shoals, Ala. / Muscle Shoals
40	Joshua McMillon	LB	6-3	240	Gr.	Memphis, Tenn. / Whitehaven

	Name	Pos.	Ht.	Wt.	Year	Hometown/H.S. Last School
41	Chris Braswell	LB	6-3	220	Fr.	Baltimore, Md. / St. Frances Academy
42	Jaylen Moody	LB	6-2	225	Jr.	Conway, S.C. / Conway
42	Sam Reed	WR	6-1	165	So.	Mountain Brook, Ala. / John Carroll
43	Jordan Smith	LB	5-10	210	Fr.	Chelsea, Ala. / Chelsea
45	Thomas Fletcher	SN	6-2	231	Sr.	Georgetown, Texas / IMG Academy
46	Melvin Billingsley	TE	6-3	230	Jr.	Opelika, Ala. / Opelika
46	Christian Swann	DB	5-9	179	Sr.	Mableton, Ga. / Pebblebrook
47	Byron Young	DL	6-3	292	So.	Laurel, Miss. / West Jones
48	Phidarian Mathis	DL	6-4	312	R-Jr.	Wisner, La. / Neville
49	Julian Lowenstein	LB	6-0	201	R-Fr.	Sarasota, Fla. / Riverview
50	Gabe Pugh	SN	6-5	273	R-Fr.	Tuscaloosa, Ala. / Northridge
50	Tim Smith	DL	6-4	320	Fr.	Sebastian, Fla. / Sebastian River
51	Tanner Bowles	OL	6-5	293	R-Fr.	Glasgow, Ky. / Glasgow
51	Robert Ellis	LB	6-0	220	Fr.	Enterprise, Ala. / Enterprise
52	Braylen Ingraham	DL	6-4	289	R-Fr.	Fort Lauderdale, Fla. / St. Thomas Aquinas
53	Matthew Barnhill	LB	6-1	209	So.	Woodway, Texas / Midway
54	Kyle Flood Jr.	LB	6-0	209	Fr.	Middlesex, N.J. / St. Joseph
55	Emil Ekiyor Jr.	OL	6-3	324	R-So.	Indianapolis, Ind. / Cathedral
56	Seth McLaughlin	OL	6-4	280	Fr.	Buford, Ga. / Buford
56	Charlie Skehan	LB	6-1	232	Fr.	Columbia, S.C. / Cardinal Newman
57	Javion Cohen	OL	6-4	325	Fr.	Phenix City, Ala. / Central
57	Joe Donald	LB	6-3	216	R-Sr.	Mountain Brook, Ala. / Mountain Brook
58	Christian Barmore	DL	6-5	310	R-So.	Philadelphia, Pa. / Neumann Goretti
59	Jake Hall	SN	6-3	238	R-So.	Saraland, Ala. / Saraland
59	Bennett Whisenhunt	LB	6-1	222	Fr.	Vestavia Hills, Ala. / Vestavia Hills
62	Jackson Roby	OL	6-5	285	Jr.	Huntsville, Ala. / Huntsville
65	Deonte Brown	OL	6-4	350	R-Sr.	Decatur, Ala. / Austin
66	Brandon Cade	OL	6-2	264	Fr.	Birmingham, Ala. / Minor
67	Donovan Hardin	OL	6-3	285	Fr.	Dublin, Ohio / Dublin Scioto
68	Alajujuan Sparks Jr.	OL	6-4	345	Fr.	Hoover, Ala. / Hoover
69	Landon Dickerson	OL	6-6	325	R-Sr.	Hickory, N.C. Florida State
70	Alex Leatherwood	OL	6-6	312	Sr.	Pensacola, Fla. / Booker T. Washington
71	Darrian Dalcourt	OL	6-3	300	So.	Havre de Grace, Md. / St. Frances Academy
72	Pierce Quick	OL	6-5	280	R-Fr.	Trussville, Ala. / Hewitt-Trussville
73	Evan Neal	OL	6-7	360	So.	Okeechobee, Fla. / IMG Academy
74	Damieon George Jr.	OL	6-6	345	Fr.	Houston, Texas / North Shore
75	Tommy Brown	OL	6-7	320	R-So.	Santa Ana, Calif. / Mater Dei
78	Amari Kight	OL	6-7	318	R-Fr.	Alabaster, Ala. / Thompson
79	Chris Owens	OL	6-3	315	R-Sr.	Arlington, Texas / Lamar
80	Michael Parker	TE	6-6	232	Fr.	Huntsville, Ala. / Westminster Christian
81	Cameron Latu	TE	6-5	250	R-So.	Salt Lake City, Utah / Olympus
82	Chase Allen	PK	6-2	188	Fr.	Colleyville, Texas / Colleyville Heritage
83	Richard Hunt	TE	6-7	235	R-Fr.	Memphis, Tenn. / Briarcrest Christian
84	Joshua Lanier	WR	5-11	160	R-Sr.	Tuscaloosa, Ala. North Alabama
85	Drew Kobayashi	WR	6-2	200	R-Sr.	Honolulu, Hawai'i Washington State
85	Charlie Scott	P	6-1	195	Sr.	Greenwood Village, Colo. Air Force
85/60	Kendall Randolph	TE/OL	6-4	298	R-Jr.	Madison, Ala. / Bob Jones
86	Carl Tucker	TE	6-2	248	Sr.	Concord, N.C. North Carolina
87	Miller Forristall	TE	6-5	244	R-Sr.	Cartersville, Ala. / Cartersville
88	Major Tennison	TE	6-5	252	R-Jr.	Flint, Texas / Bullard
89	Grant Krieger	WR	6-2	192	So.	Pittsburgh, Pa. / Pine-Richland
89	Kyle Mann	DL	6-0	270	Fr.	Powder Springs, Ga. / McEachern
90	Stephon Wynn Jr.	DL	6-4	310	R-So.	Anderson, S.C. / IMG Academy
91	Gavin Reeder	DL	6-0	292	R-Fr.	Charlotte, N.C. / Providence
92	Justin Eboigbe	DL	6-5	285	So.	Forest Park, Ga. / Forest Park
93	Jah-Marien Latham	DL	6-3	285	Fr.	Reform, Ala. / Pickens County
93	Tripp Slyman	PK/P	6-1	180	R-So.	Huntsville, Ala. / Randolph
94	DJ Dale	DL	6-3	307	So.	Birmingham, Ala. / Clay-Chalkville
95	Jack Martin	P	6-0	206	So.	Mobile, Ala. / McGill-Toolen
96	Landon Bothwell	DL	5-11	220	R-So.	Oneonta, Ala. Culver-Stockton
97	Joseph Bulovas	PK	6-0	215	R-Fr.	Mandeville, La. / Mandeville
97	LT Ikner	DL	6-4	261	Jr.	Daphne, Ala. / Daphne Hutchinson C.C.
98	Jamil Burroughs	DL	6-3	326	Fr.	Powder Springs, Ga. / McEachern
98	Sam Johnson	P	6-3	215	Fr.	Birmingham, Ala. / Oak Mountain
99	Ty Perine	P/PK	6-1	218	So.	Prattville, Ala. / Prattville